Greenwich Summer Catamaran Wine Tasting Journal

(For any time of the year)

WINDSURF PUBLISHING LLC

This journal belongs to:

_____

Also be sure to check out Windsurf Publishing's other titles on Amazon.com

All rights reserved. No part of this book may be reproduced, stored in a retrieval system, or transmitted in any form by any means, electronic, mechanical, photocopying, recording, or otherwise, without the permission of the publisher.

Published by Windsurf Publishing LLC
Greenwich, Connecticut
Copyright © Windsurf Publishing LLC
ISBN: 978-1-936509-24-9

Greenwich Summer Catamaran Wine Tasting Journal
(For any time of the year)

Date _____

Wine's Name _____

Wine's Producer _____

Winery/Vineyard Location _____

Vintage Year _____

Appearance _____

Aroma _____

Body _____

Taste _____

Finish _____

Would/Does Pair Nicely With _____

Overall Rating From 1-10 _____   Try Again? Yes No

Additional Notes:

_____

_____

_____

_____

Greenwich Summer Catamaran Wine Tasting Journal

(For any time of the year)

Date _____

Wine's Name _____

Wine's Producer _____

Winery/Vineyard Location _____

Vintage Year _____

Appearance _____

Aroma _____

Body _____

Taste _____

Finish _____

Would/Does Pair Nicely With _____

Overall Rating From 1-10 _____   Try Again? Yes No

Additional Notes:

_____

_____

_____

_____

_____

Greenwich Summer Catamaran Wine Tasting Journal
(For any time of the year)

Date _____

Wine's Name _____

Wine's Producer _____

Winery/Vineyard Location _____

Vintage Year _____

Appearance _____

Aroma _____

Body _____

Taste _____

Finish _____

Would/Does Pair Nicely With _____

Overall Rating From 1-10 _____   Try Again? Yes No

Additional Notes:

_____

_____

_____

_____

_____

Greenwich Summer Catamaran Wine Tasting Journal
(For any time of the year)

Date _____
Wine's Name _____
Wine's Producer _____
Winery/Vineyard Location _____
Vintage Year _____
Appearance _____
Aroma _____
Body _____
Taste _____
Finish _____
Would/Does Pair Nicely With _____
Overall Rating From 1-10 _____   Try Again? Yes No
Additional Notes:
_____
_____
_____
_____
_____

Greenwich Summer Catamaran Wine Tasting Journal
(For any time of the year)

Date _____

Wine's Name _____

Wine's Producer _____

Winery/Vineyard Location _____

Vintage Year _____

Appearance _____

Aroma _____

Body _____

Taste _____

Finish _____

Would/Does Pair Nicely With _____

Overall Rating From 1-10 _____   Try Again? Yes No

Additional Notes:

_____

_____

_____

_____

_____

Greenwich Summer Catamaran Wine Tasting Journal
(For any time of the year)

Date _____

Wine's Name _____

Wine's Producer _____

Winery/Vineyard Location _____

Vintage Year _____

Appearance _____

Aroma _____

Body _____

Taste _____

Finish _____

Would/Does Pair Nicely With _____

Overall Rating From 1-10 _____   Try Again? Yes No

Additional Notes:

_____
_____
_____
_____
_____
_____

Greenwich Summer Catamaran Wine Tasting Journal
(For any time of the year)

Date _____
Wine's Name _____
Wine's Producer _____
Winery/Vineyard Location _____
Vintage Year _____
Appearance _____
Aroma _____
Body _____
Taste _____
Finish _____
Would/Does Pair Nicely With _____
Overall Rating From 1-10 _____   Try Again? Yes No

Additional Notes:

_____
_____
_____
_____
_____

Greenwich Summer Catamaran Wine Tasting Journal
(For any time of the year)

Date _____

Wine's Name _____

Wine's Producer _____

Winery/Vineyard Location _____

Vintage Year _____

Appearance _____

Aroma _____

Body _____

Taste _____

Finish _____

Would/Does Pair Nicely With _____

Overall Rating From 1-10 _____   Try Again? Yes No

Additional Notes:

_____

_____

_____

_____

_____

Greenwich Summer Catamaran Wine Tasting Journal
(For any time of the year)

Date _____

Wine's Name _____

Wine's Producer _____

Winery/Vineyard Location _____

Vintage Year _____

Appearance _____

Aroma _____

Body _____

Taste _____

Finish _____

Would/Does Pair Nicely With _____

Overall Rating From 1-10 _____   Try Again? Yes No

Additional Notes:

_____

_____

_____

_____

_____

Greenwich Summer Catamaran Wine Tasting Journal
(For any time of the year)

Date _____

Wine's Name _____

Wine's Producer _____

Winery/Vineyard Location _____

Vintage Year _____

Appearance _____

Aroma _____

Body _____

Taste _____

Finish _____

Would/Does Pair Nicely With _____

Overall Rating From 1-10 _____   Try Again? Yes No

Additional Notes:

_____

_____

_____

_____

_____

Greenwich Summer Catamaran Wine Tasting Journal
(For any time of the year)

Date _____
Wine's Name _____
Wine's Producer _____
Winery/Vineyard Location _____
Vintage Year _____
Appearance _____
Aroma _____
Body _____
Taste _____
Finish _____
Would/Does Pair Nicely With _____
Overall Rating From 1-10 _____   Try Again? Yes No

Additional Notes:

_____

_____

_____

_____

_____

Greenwich Summer Catamaran Wine Tasting Journal
(For any time of the year)

Date _____

Wine's Name _____

Wine's Producer _____

Winery/Vineyard Location _____

Vintage Year _____

Appearance _____

Aroma _____

Body _____

Taste _____

Finish _____

Would/Does Pair Nicely With _____

Overall Rating From 1-10 _____   Try Again? Yes No

Additional Notes:

_____

_____

_____

_____

_____

Greenwich Summer Catamaran Wine Tasting Journal

(For any time of the year)

Date _____

Wine's Name _____

Wine's Producer _____

Winery/Vineyard Location _____

Vintage Year _____

Appearance _____

Aroma _____

Body _____

Taste _____

Finish _____

Would/Does Pair Nicely With _____

Overall Rating From 1-10 _____   Try Again? Yes No

Additional Notes:

_____

_____

_____

_____

_____

Greenwich Summer Catamaran Wine Tasting Journal
(For any time of the year)

Date _____

Wine's Name _____

Wine's Producer _____

Winery/Vineyard Location _____

Vintage Year _____

Appearance _____

Aroma _____

Body _____

Taste _____

Finish _____

Would/Does Pair Nicely With _____

Overall Rating From 1-10 _____   Try Again? Yes No

Additional Notes:

_____

_____

_____

_____

_____

Greenwich Summer Catamaran Wine Tasting Journal
(For any time of the year)

Date _____

Wine's Name _____

Wine's Producer _____

Winery/Vineyard Location _____

Vintage Year _____

Appearance _____

Aroma _____

Body _____

Taste _____

Finish _____

Would/Does Pair Nicely With _____

Overall Rating From 1-10 _____   Try Again? Yes No

Additional Notes:

_____

_____

_____

_____

_____

_____

Greenwich Summer Catamaran Wine Tasting Journal
(For any time of the year)

Date _____
Wine's Name _____
Wine's Producer _____
Winery/Vineyard Location _____
Vintage Year _____
Appearance _____
Aroma _____
Body _____
Taste _____
Finish _____
Would/Does Pair Nicely With _____
Overall Rating From 1-10 _____   Try Again? Yes No

Additional Notes:

_____
_____
_____
_____
_____
_____

Greenwich Summer Catamaran Wine Tasting Journal
(For any time of the year)

Date _____

Wine's Name _____

Wine's Producer _____

Winery/Vineyard Location _____

Vintage Year _____

Appearance _____

Aroma _____

Body _____

Taste _____

Finish _____

Would/Does Pair Nicely With _____

Overall Rating From 1-10 _____   Try Again? Yes No

Additional Notes:

_____

_____

_____

_____

_____

Greenwich Summer Catamaran Wine Tasting Journal
(For any time of the year)

Date _____

Wine's Name _____

Wine's Producer _____

Winery/Vineyard Location _____

Vintage Year _____

Appearance _____

Aroma _____

Body _____

Taste _____

Finish _____

Would/Does Pair Nicely With _____

Overall Rating From 1-10 _____   Try Again? Yes No

Additional Notes:

_____

_____

_____

_____

_____

Greenwich Summer Catamaran Wine Tasting Journal
(For any time of the year)

Date _____
Wine's Name _____
Wine's Producer _____
Winery/Vineyard Location _____
Vintage Year _____
Appearance _____
Aroma _____
Body _____
Taste _____
Finish _____
Would/Does Pair Nicely With _____
Overall Rating From 1-10 _____   Try Again? Yes No

Additional Notes:

_____
_____
_____
_____
_____
_____

Greenwich Summer Catamaran Wine Tasting Journal
(For any time of the year)

Date _____

Wine's Name _____

Wine's Producer _____

Winery/Vineyard Location _____

Vintage Year _____

Appearance _____

Aroma _____

Body _____

Taste _____

Finish _____

Would/Does Pair Nicely With _____

Overall Rating From 1-10 _____   Try Again? Yes No

Additional Notes:

_____

_____

_____

_____

_____

Greenwich Summer Catamaran Wine Tasting Journal
(For any time of the year)

Date _____

Wine's Name _____

Wine's Producer _____

Winery/Vineyard Location _____

Vintage Year _____

Appearance _____

Aroma _____

Body _____

Taste _____

Finish _____

Would/Does Pair Nicely With _____

Overall Rating From 1-10 _____   Try Again? Yes No

Additional Notes:

_____

_____

_____

_____

_____

_____

Greenwich Summer Catamaran Wine Tasting Journal
(For any time of the year)

Date _____

Wine's Name _____

Wine's Producer _____

Winery/Vineyard Location _____

Vintage Year _____

Appearance _____

Aroma _____

Body _____

Taste _____

Finish _____

Would/Does Pair Nicely With _____

Overall Rating From 1-10 _____   Try Again? Yes No

Additional Notes:

_____

_____

_____

_____

_____

Greenwich Summer Catamaran Wine Tasting Journal

(For any time of the year)

Date _____

Wine's Name _____

Wine's Producer _____

Winery/Vineyard Location _____

Vintage Year _____

Appearance _____

Aroma _____

Body _____

Taste _____

Finish _____

Would/Does Pair Nicely With _____

Overall Rating From 1-10 _____   Try Again? Yes No

Additional Notes:

_____

_____

_____

_____

_____

Greenwich Summer Catamaran Wine Tasting Journal
(For any time of the year)

Date _____

Wine's Name _____

Wine's Producer _____

Winery/Vineyard Location _____

Vintage Year _____

Appearance _____

Aroma _____

Body _____

Taste _____

Finish _____

Would/Does Pair Nicely With _____

Overall Rating From 1-10 _____   Try Again? Yes No

Additional Notes:

_____
_____
_____
_____
_____

Greenwich Summer Catamaran Wine Tasting Journal
(For any time of the year)

Date _____
Wine's Name _____
Wine's Producer _____
Winery/Vineyard Location _____
Vintage Year _____
Appearance _____
Aroma _____
Body _____
Taste _____
Finish _____
Would/Does Pair Nicely With _____
Overall Rating From 1-10 _____   Try Again? Yes No

Additional Notes:

_____
_____
_____
_____
_____

Greenwich Summer Catamaran Wine Tasting Journal
(For any time of the year)

Date _____
Wine's Name _____
Wine's Producer _____
Winery/Vineyard Location _____
Vintage Year _____
Appearance _____
Aroma _____
Body _____
Taste _____
Finish _____
Would/Does Pair Nicely With _____
Overall Rating From 1-10 _____   Try Again? Yes No

Additional Notes:

_____
_____
_____
_____
_____
_____

Greenwich Summer Catamaran Wine Tasting Journal
(For any time of the year)

Date _____

Wine's Name _____

Wine's Producer _____

Winery/Vineyard Location _____

Vintage Year _____

Appearance _____

Aroma _____

Body _____

Taste _____

Finish _____

Would/Does Pair Nicely With _____

Overall Rating From 1-10 _____   Try Again? Yes No

Additional Notes:

_____

_____

_____

_____

_____

Greenwich Summer Catamaran Wine Tasting Journal
(For any time of the year)

Date _____

Wine's Name _____

Wine's Producer _____

Winery/Vineyard Location _____

Vintage Year _____

Appearance _____

Aroma _____

Body _____

Taste _____

Finish _____

Would/Does Pair Nicely With _____

Overall Rating From 1-10 _____   Try Again? Yes No

Additional Notes:

_____

_____

_____

_____

_____

_____

Greenwich Summer Catamaran Wine Tasting Journal
(For any time of the year)

Date _____
Wine's Name _____
Wine's Producer _____
Winery/Vineyard Location _____
Vintage Year _____
Appearance _____
Aroma _____
Body _____
Taste _____
Finish _____
Would/Does Pair Nicely With _____
Overall Rating From 1-10 _____   Try Again? Yes No

Additional Notes:

_____

_____

_____

_____

Greenwich Summer Catamaran Wine Tasting Journal
(For any time of the year)

Date _____

Wine's Name _____

Wine's Producer _____

Winery/Vineyard Location _____

Vintage Year _____

Appearance _____

Aroma _____

Body _____

Taste _____

Finish _____

Would/Does Pair Nicely With _____

Overall Rating From 1-10 _____   Try Again? Yes No

Additional Notes:

_____

_____

_____

_____

_____

Greenwich Summer Catamaran Wine Tasting Journal
(For any time of the year)

Date _____

Wine's Name _____

Wine's Producer _____

Winery/Vineyard Location _____

Vintage Year _____

Appearance _____

Aroma _____

Body _____

Taste _____

Finish _____

Would/Does Pair Nicely With _____

Overall Rating From 1–10 _____   Try Again? Yes No

Additional Notes:

_____

_____

_____

_____

_____

Greenwich Summer Catamaran Wine Tasting Journal
(For any time of the year)

Date _____
Wine's Name _____
Wine's Producer _____
Winery/Vineyard Location _____
Vintage Year _____
Appearance _____
Aroma _____
Body _____
Taste _____
Finish _____
Would/Does Pair Nicely With _____
Overall Rating From 1-10 _____   Try Again? Yes No

Additional Notes:

_____
_____
_____
_____
_____

Greenwich Summer Catamaran Wine Tasting Journal
(For any time of the year)

Date _____

Wine's Name _____

Wine's Producer _____

Winery/Vineyard Location _____

Vintage Year _____

Appearance _____

Aroma _____

Body _____

Taste _____

Finish _____

Would/Does Pair Nicely With _____

Overall Rating From 1-10 _____   Try Again? Yes No

Additional Notes:

_____

_____

_____

_____

_____

_____

Greenwich Summer Catamaran Wine Tasting Journal
(For any time of the year)

Date _____

Wine's Name _____

Wine's Producer _____

Winery/Vineyard Location _____

Vintage Year _____

Appearance _____

Aroma _____

Body _____

Taste _____

Finish _____

Would/Does Pair Nicely With _____

Overall Rating From 1-10 _____   Try Again? Yes No

Additional Notes:

_____

_____

_____

_____

_____

Greenwich Summer Catamaran Wine Tasting Journal
(For any time of the year)

Date _____
Wine's Name _____
Wine's Producer _____
Winery/Vineyard Location _____
Vintage Year _____
Appearance _____
Aroma _____
Body _____
Taste _____
Finish _____
Would/Does Pair Nicely With _____
Overall Rating From 1-10 _____   Try Again? Yes No

Additional Notes:

_____
_____
_____
_____
_____
_____

Greenwich Summer Catamaran Wine Tasting Journal
(For any time of the year)

Date _____

Wine's Name _____

Wine's Producer _____

Winery/Vineyard Location _____

Vintage Year _____

Appearance _____

Aroma _____

Body _____

Taste _____

Finish _____

Would/Does Pair Nicely With _____

Overall Rating From 1-10 _____   Try Again? Yes No

Additional Notes:

_____
_____
_____
_____
_____

Greenwich Summer Catamaran Wine Tasting Journal
(For any time of the year)

Date _____
Wine's Name _____
Wine's Producer _____
Winery/Vineyard Location _____
Vintage Year _____
Appearance _____
Aroma _____
Body _____
Taste _____
Finish _____
Would/Does Pair Nicely With _____
Overall Rating From 1-10 _____   Try Again? Yes No

Additional Notes:

_____
_____
_____
_____
_____

Greenwich Summer Catamaran Wine Tasting Journal

(For any time of the year)

Date _____
Wine's Name _____
Wine's Producer _____
Winery/Vineyard Location _____
Vintage Year _____
Appearance _____
Aroma _____
Body _____
Taste _____
Finish _____
Would/Does Pair Nicely With _____
Overall Rating From 1-10 _____   Try Again? Yes No

Additional Notes:

_____
_____
_____
_____
_____

Greenwich Summer Catamaran Wine Tasting Journal
(For any time of the year)

Date _____

Wine's Name _____

Wine's Producer _____

Winery/Vineyard Location _____

Vintage Year _____

Appearance _____

Aroma _____

Body _____

Taste _____

Finish _____

Would/Does Pair Nicely With _____

Overall Rating From 1-10 _____   Try Again? Yes No

Additional Notes:

_____

_____

_____

_____

_____

Greenwich Summer Catamaran Wine Tasting Journal
(For any time of the year)

Date _____

Wine's Name _____

Wine's Producer _____

Winery/Vineyard Location _____

Vintage Year _____

Appearance _____

Aroma _____

Body _____

Taste _____

Finish _____

Would/Does Pair Nicely With _____

Overall Rating From 1-10 _____   Try Again? Yes No

Additional Notes:

_____

_____

_____

_____

_____

_____

Greenwich Summer Catamaran Wine Tasting Journal
(For any time of the year)

Date _____

Wine's Name _____

Wine's Producer _____

Winery/Vineyard Location _____

Vintage Year _____

Appearance _____

Aroma _____

Body _____

Taste _____

Finish _____

Would/Does Pair Nicely With _____

Overall Rating From 1-10 _____   Try Again? Yes No

Additional Notes:

_____

_____

_____

_____

_____

Greenwich Summer Catamaran Wine Tasting Journal
(For any time of the year)

Date _____

Wine's Name _____

Wine's Producer _____

Winery/Vineyard Location _____

Vintage Year _____

Appearance _____

Aroma _____

Body _____

Taste _____

Finish _____

Would/Does Pair Nicely With _____

Overall Rating From 1-10 _____   Try Again? Yes No

Additional Notes:

_____
_____
_____
_____
_____

Greenwich Summer Catamaran Wine Tasting Journal
(For any time of the year)

Date _____

Wine's Name _____

Wine's Producer _____

Winery/Vineyard Location _____

Vintage Year _____

Appearance _____

Aroma _____

Body _____

Taste _____

Finish _____

Would/Does Pair Nicely With _____

Overall Rating From 1-10 _____   Try Again? Yes No

Additional Notes:

_____

_____

_____

_____

_____

Greenwich Summer Catamaran Wine Tasting Journal
(For any time of the year)

Date _____

Wine's Name _____

Wine's Producer _____

Winery/Vineyard Location _____

Vintage Year _____

Appearance _____

Aroma _____

Body _____

Taste _____

Finish _____

Would/Does Pair Nicely With _____

Overall Rating From 1-10 _____   Try Again? Yes No

Additional Notes:

_____

_____

_____

_____

_____

_____

Greenwich Summer Catamaran Wine Tasting Journal
(For any time of the year)

Date _____

Wine's Name _____

Wine's Producer _____

Winery/Vineyard Location _____

Vintage Year _____

Appearance _____

Aroma _____

Body _____

Taste _____

Finish _____

Would/Does Pair Nicely With _____

Overall Rating From 1-10 _____   Try Again? Yes No

Additional Notes:

_____

_____

_____

_____

_____

Greenwich Summer Catamaran Wine Tasting Journal
(For any time of the year)

Date _____

Wine's Name _____

Wine's Producer _____

Winery/Vineyard Location _____

Vintage Year _____

Appearance _____

Aroma _____

Body _____

Taste _____

Finish _____

Would/Does Pair Nicely With _____

Overall Rating From 1-10 _____   Try Again? Yes No

Additional Notes:

_____

_____

_____

_____

_____

Greenwich Summer Catamaran Wine Tasting Journal
(For any time of the year)

Date _____

Wine's Name _____

Wine's Producer _____

Winery/Vineyard Location _____

Vintage Year _____

Appearance _____

Aroma _____

Body _____

Taste _____

Finish _____

Would/Does Pair Nicely With _____

Overall Rating From 1-10 _____   Try Again? Yes No

Additional Notes:

_____

_____

_____

_____

_____

Greenwich Summer Catamaran Wine Tasting Journal
(For any time of the year)

Date _____

Wine's Name _____

Wine's Producer _____

Winery/Vineyard Location _____

Vintage Year _____

Appearance _____

Aroma _____

Body _____

Taste _____

Finish _____

Would/Does Pair Nicely With _____

Overall Rating From 1-10 _____   Try Again? Yes No

Additional Notes:

_____

_____

_____

_____

_____

Greenwich Summer Catamaran Wine Tasting Journal

(For any time of the year)

Date _____

Wine's Name _____

Wine's Producer _____

Winery/Vineyard Location _____

Vintage Year _____

Appearance _____

Aroma _____

Body _____

Taste _____

Finish _____

Would/Does Pair Nicely With _____

Overall Rating From 1-10 _____   Try Again? Yes No

Additional Notes:

_____

_____

_____

_____

_____

Greenwich Summer Catamaran Wine Tasting Journal
(For any time of the year)

Date _____

Wine's Name _____

Wine's Producer _____

Winery/Vineyard Location _____

Vintage Year _____

Appearance _____

Aroma _____

Body _____

Taste _____

Finish _____

Would/Does Pair Nicely With _____

Overall Rating From 1-10 _____   Try Again? Yes No

Additional Notes:

_____

_____

_____

_____

_____

Greenwich Summer Catamaran Wine Tasting Journal
(For any time of the year)

Date _____

Wine's Name _____

Wine's Producer _____

Winery/Vineyard Location _____

Vintage Year _____

Appearance _____

Aroma _____

Body _____

Taste _____

Finish _____

Would/Does Pair Nicely With _____

Overall Rating From 1-10 _____   Try Again? Yes No

Additional Notes:

_____

_____

_____

_____

_____

_____

Greenwich Summer Catamaran Wine Tasting Journal
(For any time of the year)

Date _____
Wine's Name _____
Wine's Producer _____
Winery/Vineyard Location _____
Vintage Year _____
Appearance _____
Aroma _____
Body _____
Taste _____
Finish _____
Would/Does Pair Nicely With _____
Overall Rating From 1-10 _____   Try Again? Yes No

Additional Notes:

_____
_____
_____
_____
_____
_____

Greenwich Summer Catamaran Wine Tasting Journal
(For any time of the year)

Date _____

Wine's Name _____

Wine's Producer _____

Winery/Vineyard Location _____

Vintage Year _____

Appearance _____

Aroma _____

Body _____

Taste _____

Finish _____

Would/Does Pair Nicely With _____

Overall Rating From 1-10 _____   Try Again? Yes No

Additional Notes:

_____

_____

_____

_____

_____

Greenwich Summer Catamaran Wine Tasting Journal
(For any time of the year)

Date _____

Wine's Name _____

Wine's Producer _____

Winery/Vineyard Location _____

Vintage Year _____

Appearance _____

Aroma _____

Body _____

Taste _____

Finish _____

Would/Does Pair Nicely With _____

Overall Rating From 1-10 _____   Try Again? Yes No

Additional Notes:

_____

_____

_____

_____

Greenwich Summer Catamaran Wine Tasting Journal
(For any time of the year)

Date _____
Wine's Name _____
Wine's Producer _____
Winery/Vineyard Location _____
Vintage Year _____
Appearance _____
Aroma _____
Body _____
Taste _____
Finish _____
Would/Does Pair Nicely With _____
Overall Rating From 1-10 _____   Try Again? Yes No

Additional Notes:

_____
_____
_____
_____
_____

Greenwich Summer Catamaran Wine Tasting Journal
(For any time of the year)

Date _____

Wine's Name _____

Wine's Producer _____

Winery/Vineyard Location _____

Vintage Year _____

Appearance _____

Aroma _____

Body _____

Taste _____

Finish _____

Would/Does Pair Nicely With _____

Overall Rating From 1-10 _____   Try Again? Yes No

Additional Notes:

_____

_____

_____

_____

_____

Greenwich Summer Catamaran Wine Tasting Journal
(For any time of the year)

Date _____

Wine's Name _____

Wine's Producer _____

Winery/Vineyard Location _____

Vintage Year _____

Appearance _____

Aroma _____

Body _____

Taste _____

Finish _____

Would/Does Pair Nicely With _____

Overall Rating From 1-10 _____   Try Again? Yes No

Additional Notes:

_____

_____

_____

_____

_____

Greenwich Summer Catamaran Wine Tasting Journal
(For any time of the year)

Date _____

Wine's Name _____

Wine's Producer _____

Winery/Vineyard Location _____

Vintage Year _____

Appearance _____

Aroma _____

Body _____

Taste _____

Finish _____

Would/Does Pair Nicely With _____

Overall Rating From 1-10 _____   Try Again? Yes No

Additional Notes:

_____

_____

_____

_____

_____

_____

Greenwich Summer Catamaran Wine Tasting Journal

(For any time of the year)

Date _____
Wine's Name _____
Wine's Producer _____
Winery/Vineyard Location _____
Vintage Year _____
Appearance _____
Aroma _____
Body _____
Taste _____
Finish _____
Would/Does Pair Nicely With _____
Overall Rating From 1-10 _____   Try Again? Yes No

Additional Notes:

_____
_____
_____
_____
_____

Greenwich Summer Catamaran Wine Tasting Journal
(For any time of the year)

Date _____

Wine's Name _____

Wine's Producer _____

Winery/Vineyard Location _____

Vintage Year _____

Appearance _____

Aroma _____

Body _____

Taste _____

Finish _____

Would/Does Pair Nicely With _____

Overall Rating From 1-10 _____   Try Again? Yes No

Additional Notes:

_____

_____

_____

_____

_____

Greenwich Summer Catamaran Wine Tasting Journal
(For any time of the year)

Date _____
Wine's Name _____
Wine's Producer _____
Winery/Vineyard Location _____
Vintage Year _____
Appearance _____
Aroma _____
Body _____
Taste _____
Finish _____
Would/Does Pair Nicely With _____
Overall Rating From 1-10 _____   Try Again? Yes No

Additional Notes:

_____

_____

_____

_____

_____

Greenwich Summer Catamaran Wine Tasting Journal
(For any time of the year)

Date _____
Wine's Name _____
Wine's Producer _____
Winery/Vineyard Location _____
Vintage Year _____
Appearance _____
Aroma _____
Body _____
Taste _____
Finish _____
Would/Does Pair Nicely With _____
Overall Rating From 1-10 _____   Try Again? Yes No

Additional Notes:

_____
_____
_____
_____
_____
_____

Greenwich Summer Catamaran Wine Tasting Journal
(For any time of the year)

Date _____

Wine's Name _____

Wine's Producer _____

Winery/Vineyard Location _____

Vintage Year _____

Appearance _____

Aroma _____

Body _____

Taste _____

Finish _____

Would/Does Pair Nicely With _____

Overall Rating From 1-10 _____   Try Again? Yes No

Additional Notes:

_____

_____

_____

_____

_____

Greenwich Summer Catamaran Wine Tasting Journal
(For any time of the year)

Date _____

Wine's Name _____

Wine's Producer _____

Winery/Vineyard Location _____

Vintage Year _____

Appearance _____

Aroma _____

Body _____

Taste _____

Finish _____

Would/Does Pair Nicely With _____

Overall Rating From 1-10 _____   Try Again? Yes No

Additional Notes:

_____

_____

_____

_____

_____

Greenwich Summer Catamaran Wine Tasting Journal
(For any time of the year)

Date _____
Wine's Name _____
Wine's Producer _____
Winery/Vineyard Location _____
Vintage Year _____
Appearance _____
Aroma _____
Body _____
Taste _____
Finish _____
Would/Does Pair Nicely With _____
Overall Rating From 1-10 _____   Try Again? Yes No

Additional Notes:

_____
_____
_____
_____
_____
_____

Greenwich Summer Catamaran Wine Tasting Journal
(For any time of the year)

Date _____

Wine's Name _____

Wine's Producer _____

Winery/Vineyard Location _____

Vintage Year _____

Appearance _____

Aroma _____

Body _____

Taste _____

Finish _____

Would/Does Pair Nicely With _____

Overall Rating From 1-10 _____   Try Again? Yes No

Additional Notes:

_____

_____

_____

_____

_____

Greenwich Summer Catamaran Wine Tasting Journal
(For any time of the year)

Date _____
Wine's Name _____
Wine's Producer _____
Winery/Vineyard Location _____
Vintage Year _____
Appearance _____
Aroma _____
Body _____
Taste _____
Finish _____
Would/Does Pair Nicely With _____
Overall Rating From 1-10 _____   Try Again? Yes No

Additional Notes:

_____
_____
_____
_____
_____

Greenwich Summer Catamaran Wine Tasting Journal
(For any time of the year)

Date _____

Wine's Name _____

Wine's Producer _____

Winery/Vineyard Location _____

Vintage Year _____

Appearance _____

Aroma _____

Body _____

Taste _____

Finish _____

Would/Does Pair Nicely With _____

Overall Rating From 1-10 _____   Try Again? Yes No

Additional Notes:

_____

_____

_____

_____

_____

_____

Greenwich Summer Catamaran Wine Tasting Journal
(For any time of the year)

Date _____
Wine's Name _____
Wine's Producer _____
Winery/Vineyard Location _____
Vintage Year _____
Appearance _____
Aroma _____
Body _____
Taste _____
Finish _____
Would/Does Pair Nicely With _____
Overall Rating From 1-10 _____   Try Again? Yes No

Additional Notes:

_____

_____

_____

_____

_____

_____

Greenwich Summer Catamaran Wine Tasting Journal
(For any time of the year)

Date _____

Wine's Name _____

Wine's Producer _____

Winery/Vineyard Location _____

Vintage Year _____

Appearance _____

Aroma _____

Body _____

Taste _____

Finish _____

Would/Does Pair Nicely With _____

Overall Rating From 1-10 _____   Try Again? Yes No

Additional Notes:

_____

_____

_____

_____

_____

_____

Greenwich Summer Catamaran Wine Tasting Journal
(For any time of the year)

Date _____
Wine's Name _____
Wine's Producer _____
Winery/Vineyard Location _____
Vintage Year _____
Appearance _____
Aroma _____
Body _____
Taste _____
Finish _____
Would/Does Pair Nicely With _____
Overall Rating From 1-10 _____   Try Again? Yes No

Additional Notes:

_____

_____

_____

_____

Greenwich Summer Catamaran Wine Tasting Journal
(For any time of the year)

Date _____

Wine's Name _____

Wine's Producer _____

Winery/Vineyard Location _____

Vintage Year _____

Appearance _____

Aroma _____

Body _____

Taste _____

Finish _____

Would/Does Pair Nicely With _____

Overall Rating From 1-10 _____   Try Again? Yes No

Additional Notes:

_____

_____

_____

_____

_____

Greenwich Summer Catamaran Wine Tasting Journal
(For any time of the year)

Date _____
Wine's Name _____
Wine's Producer _____
Winery/Vineyard Location _____
Vintage Year _____
Appearance _____
Aroma _____
Body _____
Taste _____
Finish _____
Would/Does Pair Nicely With _____
Overall Rating From 1-10 _____   Try Again? Yes No

Additional Notes:

_____
_____
_____
_____
_____
_____

Greenwich Summer Catamaran Wine Tasting Journal
(For any time of the year)

Date _____

Wine's Name _____

Wine's Producer _____

Winery/Vineyard Location _____

Vintage Year _____

Appearance _____

Aroma _____

Body _____

Taste _____

Finish _____

Would/Does Pair Nicely With _____

Overall Rating From 1-10 _____   Try Again? Yes No

Additional Notes:

_____

_____

_____

_____

_____

_____

Greenwich Summer Catamaran Wine Tasting Journal
(For any time of the year)

Date _____

Wine's Name _____

Wine's Producer _____

Winery/Vineyard Location _____

Vintage Year _____

Appearance _____

Aroma _____

Body _____

Taste _____

Finish _____

Would/Does Pair Nicely With _____

Overall Rating From 1-10 _____   Try Again? Yes No

Additional Notes:

_____

_____

_____

_____

_____

_____

Greenwich Summer Catamaran Wine Tasting Journal
(For any time of the year)

Date _____
Wine's Name _____
Wine's Producer _____
Winery/Vineyard Location _____
Vintage Year _____
Appearance _____
Aroma _____
Body _____
Taste _____
Finish _____
Would/Does Pair Nicely With _____
Overall Rating From 1-10 _____   Try Again? Yes No

Additional Notes:

_____
_____
_____
_____
_____
_____

Greenwich Summer Catamaran Wine Tasting Journal
(For any time of the year)

Date _____

Wine's Name _____

Wine's Producer _____

Winery/Vineyard Location _____

Vintage Year _____

Appearance _____

Aroma _____

Body _____

Taste _____

Finish _____

Would/Does Pair Nicely With _____

Overall Rating From 1-10 _____   Try Again? Yes No

Additional Notes:

_____

_____

_____

_____

_____

Greenwich Summer Catamaran Wine Tasting Journal
(For any time of the year)

Date _____

Wine's Name _____

Wine's Producer _____

Winery/Vineyard Location _____

Vintage Year _____

Appearance _____

Aroma _____

Body _____

Taste _____

Finish _____

Would/Does Pair Nicely With _____

Overall Rating From 1-10 _____   Try Again? Yes No

Additional Notes:

_____

_____

_____

_____

_____

Greenwich Summer Catamaran Wine Tasting Journal
(For any time of the year)

Date _____

Wine's Name _____

Wine's Producer _____

Winery/Vineyard Location _____

Vintage Year _____

Appearance _____

Aroma _____

Body _____

Taste _____

Finish _____

Would/Does Pair Nicely With _____

Overall Rating From 1-10 _____   Try Again? Yes No

Additional Notes:

_____

_____

_____

_____

_____

_____

Greenwich Summer Catamaran Wine Tasting Journal
(For any time of the year)

Date _____

Wine's Name _____

Wine's Producer _____

Winery/Vineyard Location _____

Vintage Year _____

Appearance _____

Aroma _____

Body _____

Taste _____

Finish _____

Would/Does Pair Nicely With _____

Overall Rating From 1-10 _____   Try Again? Yes No

Additional Notes:

_____

_____

_____

_____

_____

Greenwich Summer Catamaran Wine Tasting Journal
(For any time of the year)

Date _____
Wine's Name _____
Wine's Producer _____
Winery/Vineyard Location _____
Vintage Year _____
Appearance _____
Aroma _____
Body _____
Taste _____
Finish _____
Would/Does Pair Nicely With _____
Overall Rating From 1-10 _____   Try Again? Yes No

Additional Notes:

_____
_____
_____
_____
_____
_____

Greenwich Summer Catamaran Wine Tasting Journal
(For any time of the year)

Date _____

Wine's Name _____

Wine's Producer _____

Winery/Vineyard Location _____

Vintage Year _____

Appearance _____

Aroma _____

Body _____

Taste _____

Finish _____

Would/Does Pair Nicely With _____

Overall Rating From 1-10 _____   Try Again? Yes No

Additional Notes:

_____

_____

_____

_____

_____

Greenwich Summer Catamaran Wine Tasting Journal
(For any time of the year)

Date _____

Wine's Name _____

Wine's Producer _____

Winery/Vineyard Location _____

Vintage Year _____

Appearance _____

Aroma _____

Body _____

Taste _____

Finish _____

Would/Does Pair Nicely With _____

Overall Rating From 1-10 _____   Try Again? Yes No

Additional Notes:

_____

_____

_____

_____

_____

Greenwich Summer Catamaran Wine Tasting Journal
(For any time of the year)

Date _____

Wine's Name _____

Wine's Producer _____

Winery/Vineyard Location _____

Vintage Year _____

Appearance _____

Aroma _____

Body _____

Taste _____

Finish _____

Would/Does Pair Nicely With _____

Overall Rating From 1-10 _____   Try Again? Yes No

Additional Notes:

_____

_____

_____

_____

_____

Greenwich Summer Catamaran Wine Tasting Journal
(For any time of the year)

Date _____

Wine's Name _____

Wine's Producer _____

Winery/Vineyard Location _____

Vintage Year _____

Appearance _____

Aroma _____

Body _____

Taste _____

Finish _____

Would/Does Pair Nicely With _____

Overall Rating From 1-10 _____   Try Again? Yes No

Additional Notes:

_____

_____

_____

_____

_____

Greenwich Summer Catamaran Wine Tasting Journal

(For any time of the year)

Date _____

Wine's Name _____

Wine's Producer _____

Winery/Vineyard Location _____

Vintage Year _____

Appearance _____

Aroma _____

Body _____

Taste _____

Finish _____

Would/Does Pair Nicely With _____

Overall Rating From 1-10 _____   Try Again? Yes No

Additional Notes:

_____

_____

_____

_____

_____

_____

Greenwich Summer Catamaran Wine Tasting Journal
(For any time of the year)

Date _____

Wine's Name _____

Wine's Producer _____

Winery/Vineyard Location _____

Vintage Year _____

Appearance _____

Aroma _____

Body _____

Taste _____

Finish _____

Would/Does Pair Nicely With _____

Overall Rating From 1-10 _____   Try Again? Yes No

Additional Notes:

_____

_____

_____

_____

_____

Greenwich Summer Catamaran Wine Tasting Journal
(For any time of the year)

Date _____

Wine's Name _____

Wine's Producer _____

Winery/Vineyard Location _____

Vintage Year _____

Appearance _____

Aroma _____

Body _____

Taste _____

Finish _____

Would/Does Pair Nicely With _____

Overall Rating From 1-10 _____   Try Again? Yes No

Additional Notes:

_____

_____

_____

_____

_____

_____

Greenwich Summer Catamaran Wine Tasting Journal
(For any time of the year)

Date _____

Wine's Name _____

Wine's Producer _____

Winery/Vineyard Location _____

Vintage Year _____

Appearance _____

Aroma _____

Body _____

Taste _____

Finish _____

Would/Does Pair Nicely With _____

Overall Rating From 1-10 _____   Try Again? Yes No

Additional Notes:

_____

_____

_____

_____

_____

_____

Greenwich Summer Catamaran Wine Tasting Journal
(For any time of the year)

Date _____

Wine's Name _____

Wine's Producer _____

Winery/Vineyard Location _____

Vintage Year _____

Appearance _____

Aroma _____

Body _____

Taste _____

Finish _____

Would/Does Pair Nicely With _____

Overall Rating From 1-10 _____   Try Again? Yes No

Additional Notes:

_____

_____

_____

_____

_____

Greenwich Summer Catamaran Wine Tasting Journal
(For any time of the year)

Date _____

Wine's Name _____

Wine's Producer _____

Winery/Vineyard Location _____

Vintage Year _____

Appearance _____

Aroma _____

Body _____

Taste _____

Finish _____

Would/Does Pair Nicely With _____

Overall Rating From 1-10 _____   Try Again? Yes No

Additional Notes:

_____

_____

_____

_____

_____

Greenwich Summer Catamaran Wine Tasting Journal

(For any time of the year)

Date _____

Wine's Name _____

Wine's Producer _____

Winery/Vineyard Location _____

Vintage Year _____

Appearance _____

Aroma _____

Body _____

Taste _____

Finish _____

Would/Does Pair Nicely With _____

Overall Rating From 1-10 _____   Try Again? Yes No

Additional Notes:

_____

_____

_____

_____

_____

Greenwich Summer Catamaran Wine Tasting Journal
(For any time of the year)

Date _____
Wine's Name _____
Wine's Producer _____
Winery/Vineyard Location _____
Vintage Year _____
Appearance _____
Aroma _____
Body _____
Taste _____
Finish _____
Would/Does Pair Nicely With _____
Overall Rating From 1-10 _____   Try Again? Yes No

Additional Notes:

_____
_____
_____
_____
_____
_____

Greenwich Summer Catamaran Wine Tasting Journal
(For any time of the year)

Date _____
Wine's Name _____
Wine's Producer _____
Winery/Vineyard Location _____
Vintage Year _____
Appearance _____
Aroma _____
Body _____
Taste _____
Finish _____
Would/Does Pair Nicely With _____
Overall Rating From 1-10 _____   Try Again? Yes No
Additional Notes:

_____
_____
_____
_____
_____
_____

Greenwich Summer Catamaran Wine Tasting Journal
(For any time of the year)

Date _____

Wine's Name _____

Wine's Producer _____

Winery/Vineyard Location _____

Vintage Year _____

Appearance _____

Aroma _____

Body _____

Taste _____

Finish _____

Would/Does Pair Nicely With _____

Overall Rating From 1-10 _____   Try Again? Yes No

Additional Notes:

_____

_____

_____

_____

_____

Greenwich Summer Catamaran Wine Tasting Journal
(For any time of the year)

Date _____

Wine's Name _____

Wine's Producer _____

Winery/Vineyard Location _____

Vintage Year _____

Appearance _____

Aroma _____

Body _____

Taste _____

Finish _____

Would/Does Pair Nicely With _____

Overall Rating From 1-10 _____   Try Again? Yes No

Additional Notes:

_____

_____

_____

_____

_____

_____

Greenwich Summer Catamaran Wine Tasting Journal
(For any time of the year)

Date _____

Wine's Name _____

Wine's Producer _____

Winery/Vineyard Location _____

Vintage Year _____

Appearance _____

Aroma _____

Body _____

Taste _____

Finish _____

Would/Does Pair Nicely With _____

Overall Rating From 1-10 _____   Try Again? Yes No

Additional Notes:

_____

_____

_____

_____

_____

Greenwich Summer Catamaran Wine Tasting Journal
(For any time of the year)

Date _____

Wine's Name _____

Wine's Producer _____

Winery/Vineyard Location _____

Vintage Year _____

Appearance _____

Aroma _____

Body _____

Taste _____

Finish _____

Would/Does Pair Nicely With _____

Overall Rating From 1-10 _____   Try Again? Yes No

Additional Notes:

_____

_____

_____

_____

_____

_____

Greenwich Summer Catamaran Wine Tasting Journal
(For any time of the year)

Date _____

Wine's Name _____

Wine's Producer _____

Winery/Vineyard Location _____

Vintage Year _____

Appearance _____

Aroma _____

Body _____

Taste _____

Finish _____

Would/Does Pair Nicely With _____

Overall Rating From 1-10 _____   Try Again? Yes No

Additional Notes:

_____

_____

_____

_____

_____

_____

Greenwich Summer Catamaran Wine Tasting Journal
(For any time of the year)

Date _____

Wine's Name _____

Wine's Producer _____

Winery/Vineyard Location _____

Vintage Year _____

Appearance _____

Aroma _____

Body _____

Taste _____

Finish _____

Would/Does Pair Nicely With _____

Overall Rating From 1-10 _____   Try Again? Yes No

Additional Notes:

_____

_____

_____

_____

_____

_____

Greenwich Summer Catamaran Wine Tasting Journal
(For any time of the year)

Date _____

Wine's Name _____

Wine's Producer _____

Winery/Vineyard Location _____

Vintage Year _____

Appearance _____

Aroma _____

Body _____

Taste _____

Finish _____

Would/Does Pair Nicely With _____

Overall Rating From 1-10 _____   Try Again? Yes No

Additional Notes:

_____

_____

_____

_____

_____

Greenwich Summer Catamaran Wine Tasting Journal
(For any time of the year)

Date _____

Wine's Name _____

Wine's Producer _____

Winery/Vineyard Location _____

Vintage Year _____

Appearance _____

Aroma _____

Body _____

Taste _____

Finish _____

Would/Does Pair Nicely With _____

Overall Rating From 1-10 _____   Try Again? Yes No

Additional Notes:

_____

_____

_____

_____

_____

Greenwich Summer Catamaran Wine Tasting Journal
(For any time of the year)

Date _____
Wine's Name _____
Wine's Producer _____
Winery/Vineyard Location _____
Vintage Year _____
Appearance _____
Aroma _____
Body _____
Taste _____
Finish _____
Would/Does Pair Nicely With _____
Overall Rating From 1-10 _____   Try Again? Yes No

Additional Notes:

_____
_____
_____
_____

Greenwich Summer Catamaran Wine Tasting Journal
(For any time of the year)

Date _____

Wine's Name _____

Wine's Producer _____

Winery/Vineyard Location _____

Vintage Year _____

Appearance _____

Aroma _____

Body _____

Taste _____

Finish _____

Would/Does Pair Nicely With _____

Overall Rating From 1-10 _____   Try Again? Yes No

Additional Notes:

_____

_____

_____

_____

_____

Greenwich Summer Catamaran Wine Tasting Journal
(For any time of the year)

Date _____

Wine's Name _____

Wine's Producer _____

Winery/Vineyard Location _____

Vintage Year _____

Appearance _____

Aroma _____

Body _____

Taste _____

Finish _____

Would/Does Pair Nicely With _____

Overall Rating From 1-10 _____   Try Again? Yes No

Additional Notes:

_____

_____

_____

_____

_____

_____

Greenwich Summer Catamaran Wine Tasting Journal
(For any time of the year)

Date _____

Wine's Name _____

Wine's Producer _____

Winery/Vineyard Location _____

Vintage Year _____

Appearance _____

Aroma _____

Body _____

Taste _____

Finish _____

Would/Does Pair Nicely With _____

Overall Rating From 1-10 _____   Try Again? Yes No

Additional Notes:

_____

_____

_____

_____

_____

Greenwich Summer Catamaran Wine Tasting Journal
(For any time of the year)

Date _____

Wine's Name _____

Wine's Producer _____

Winery/Vineyard Location _____

Vintage Year _____

Appearance _____

Aroma _____

Body _____

Taste _____

Finish _____

Would/Does Pair Nicely With _____

Overall Rating From 1-10 _____   Try Again? Yes No

Additional Notes:

_____

_____

_____

_____

_____

Greenwich Summer Catamaran Wine Tasting Journal
(For any time of the year)

Date _____

Wine's Name _____

Wine's Producer _____

Winery/Vineyard Location _____

Vintage Year _____

Appearance _____

Aroma _____

Body _____

Taste _____

Finish _____

Would/Does Pair Nicely With _____

Overall Rating From 1-10 _____   Try Again? Yes No

Additional Notes:

_____
_____
_____
_____
_____

Greenwich Summer Catamaran Wine Tasting Journal
(For any time of the year)

Date _____
Wine's Name _____
Wine's Producer _____
Winery/Vineyard Location _____
Vintage Year _____
Appearance _____
Aroma _____
Body _____
Taste _____
Finish _____
Would/Does Pair Nicely With _____
Overall Rating From 1-10 _____   Try Again? Yes No

Additional Notes:

_____
_____
_____
_____
_____

Greenwich Summer Catamaran Wine Tasting Journal
(For any time of the year)

Date _____

Wine's Name _____

Wine's Producer _____

Winery/Vineyard Location _____

Vintage Year _____

Appearance _____

Aroma _____

Body _____

Taste _____

Finish _____

Would/Does Pair Nicely With _____

Overall Rating From 1-10 _____   Try Again? Yes No

Additional Notes:

_____

_____

_____

_____

_____

Greenwich Summer Catamaran Wine Tasting Journal
(For any time of the year)

Date _____

Wine's Name _____

Wine's Producer _____

Winery/Vineyard Location _____

Vintage Year _____

Appearance _____

Aroma _____

Body _____

Taste _____

Finish _____

Would/Does Pair Nicely With _____

Overall Rating From 1-10 _____   Try Again? Yes No

Additional Notes:

_____

_____

_____

_____

_____

Greenwich Summer Catamaran Wine Tasting Journal
(For any time of the year)

Date _____

Wine's Name _____

Wine's Producer _____

Winery/Vineyard Location _____

Vintage Year _____

Appearance _____

Aroma _____

Body _____

Taste _____

Finish _____

Would/Does Pair Nicely With _____

Overall Rating From 1-10 _____   Try Again? Yes No

Additional Notes:

_____

_____

_____

_____

_____

_____

Greenwich Summer Catamaran Wine Tasting Journal
(For any time of the year)

Date _____
Wine's Name _____
Wine's Producer _____
Winery/Vineyard Location _____
Vintage Year _____
Appearance _____
Aroma _____
Body _____
Taste _____
Finish _____
Would/Does Pair Nicely With _____
Overall Rating From 1-10 _____   Try Again? Yes No
Additional Notes:

_____
_____
_____
_____
_____
_____

Greenwich Summer Catamaran Wine Tasting Journal
(For any time of the year)

Date _____

Wine's Name _____

Wine's Producer _____

Winery/Vineyard Location _____

Vintage Year _____

Appearance _____

Aroma _____

Body _____

Taste _____

Finish _____

Would/Does Pair Nicely With _____

Overall Rating From 1-10 _____   Try Again? Yes No

Additional Notes:

_____

_____

_____

_____

_____

Greenwich Summer Catamaran Wine Tasting Journal
(For any time of the year)

Date _____

Wine's Name _____

Wine's Producer _____

Winery/Vineyard Location _____

Vintage Year _____

Appearance _____

Aroma _____

Body _____

Taste _____

Finish _____

Would/Does Pair Nicely With _____

Overall Rating From 1-10 _____   Try Again? Yes No

Additional Notes:

_____
_____
_____
_____
_____

Greenwich Summer Catamaran Wine Tasting Journal
(For any time of the year)

Date _____

Wine's Name _____

Wine's Producer _____

Winery/Vineyard Location _____

Vintage Year _____

Appearance _____

Aroma _____

Body _____

Taste _____

Finish _____

Would/Does Pair Nicely With _____

Overall Rating From 1-10 _____   Try Again? Yes No

Additional Notes:

_____

_____

_____

_____

_____

Greenwich Summer Catamaran Wine Tasting Journal
(For any time of the year)

Date _____
Wine's Name _____
Wine's Producer _____
Winery/Vineyard Location _____
Vintage Year _____
Appearance _____
Aroma _____
Body _____
Taste _____
Finish _____
Would/Does Pair Nicely With _____
Overall Rating From 1-10 _____   Try Again? Yes No

Additional Notes:

_____
_____
_____
_____
_____

Greenwich Summer Catamaran Wine Tasting Journal
(For any time of the year)

Date _____

Wine's Name _____

Wine's Producer _____

Winery/Vineyard Location _____

Vintage Year _____

Appearance _____

Aroma _____

Body _____

Taste _____

Finish _____

Would/Does Pair Nicely With _____

Overall Rating From 1-10 _____   Try Again? Yes No

Additional Notes:

_____

_____

_____

_____

_____

Greenwich Summer Catamaran Wine Tasting Journal
(For any time of the year)

Date _____

Wine's Name _____

Wine's Producer _____

Winery/Vineyard Location _____

Vintage Year _____

Appearance _____

Aroma _____

Body _____

Taste _____

Finish _____

Would/Does Pair Nicely With _____

Overall Rating From 1-10 _____   Try Again? Yes No

Additional Notes:

_____

_____

_____

_____

_____

Greenwich Summer Catamaran Wine Tasting Journal
(For any time of the year)

Date _____

Wine's Name _____

Wine's Producer _____

Winery/Vineyard Location _____

Vintage Year _____

Appearance _____

Aroma _____

Body _____

Taste _____

Finish _____

Would/Does Pair Nicely With _____

Overall Rating From 1-10 _____   Try Again? Yes No

Additional Notes:

_____

_____

_____

_____

_____

Greenwich Summer Catamaran Wine Tasting Journal
(For any time of the year)

Date _____

Wine's Name _____

Wine's Producer _____

Winery/Vineyard Location _____

Vintage Year _____

Appearance _____

Aroma _____

Body _____

Taste _____

Finish _____

Would/Does Pair Nicely With _____

Overall Rating From 1-10 _____   Try Again? Yes No

Additional Notes:

_____

_____

_____

_____

_____

Greenwich Summer Catamaran Wine Tasting Journal
(For any time of the year)

Date _____

Wine's Name _____

Wine's Producer _____

Winery/Vineyard Location _____

Vintage Year _____

Appearance _____

Aroma _____

Body _____

Taste _____

Finish _____

Would/Does Pair Nicely With _____

Overall Rating From 1-10 _____   Try Again? Yes No

Additional Notes:

_____

_____

_____

_____

_____

Greenwich Summer Catamaran Wine Tasting Journal
(For any time of the year)

Date _____

Wine's Name _____

Wine's Producer _____

Winery/Vineyard Location _____

Vintage Year _____

Appearance _____

Aroma _____

Body _____

Taste _____

Finish _____

Would/Does Pair Nicely With _____

Overall Rating From 1-10 _____   Try Again? Yes No

Additional Notes:

_____

_____

_____

_____

_____

Greenwich Summer Catamaran Wine Tasting Journal
(For any time of the year)

Date _____

Wine's Name _____

Wine's Producer _____

Winery/Vineyard Location _____

Vintage Year _____

Appearance _____

Aroma _____

Body _____

Taste _____

Finish _____

Would/Does Pair Nicely With _____

Overall Rating From 1-10 _____   Try Again? Yes No

Additional Notes:

_____

_____

_____

_____

_____

_____

Greenwich Summer Catamaran Wine Tasting Journal
(For any time of the year)

Date _____
Wine's Name _____
Wine's Producer _____
Winery/Vineyard Location _____
Vintage Year _____
Appearance _____
Aroma _____
Body _____
Taste _____
Finish _____
Would/Does Pair Nicely With _____
Overall Rating From 1-10 _____   Try Again? Yes No

Additional Notes:

_____
_____
_____
_____
_____
_____

Greenwich Summer Catamaran Wine Tasting Journal
(For any time of the year)

Date _____

Wine's Name _____

Wine's Producer _____

Winery/Vineyard Location _____

Vintage Year _____

Appearance _____

Aroma _____

Body _____

Taste _____

Finish _____

Would/Does Pair Nicely With _____

Overall Rating From 1-10 _____   Try Again? Yes No

Additional Notes:

_____

_____

_____

_____

_____

Greenwich Summer Catamaran Wine Tasting Journal

(For any time of the year)

Date _____

Wine's Name _____

Wine's Producer _____

Winery/Vineyard Location _____

Vintage Year _____

Appearance _____

Aroma _____

Body _____

Taste _____

Finish _____

Would/Does Pair Nicely With _____

Overall Rating From 1-10 _____   Try Again? Yes No

Additional Notes:

_____

_____

_____

_____

_____

_____

Greenwich Summer Catamaran Wine Tasting Journal
(For any time of the year)

Date _____
Wine's Name _____
Wine's Producer _____
Winery/Vineyard Location _____
Vintage Year _____
Appearance _____
Aroma _____
Body _____
Taste _____
Finish _____
Would/Does Pair Nicely With _____
Overall Rating From 1-10 _____   Try Again? Yes No
                Additional Notes:

_____
_____
_____
_____
_____

Greenwich Summer Catamaran Wine Tasting Journal
(For any time of the year)

Date _____

Wine's Name _____

Wine's Producer _____

Winery/Vineyard Location _____

Vintage Year _____

Appearance _____

Aroma _____

Body _____

Taste _____

Finish _____

Would/Does Pair Nicely With _____

Overall Rating From 1-10 _____   Try Again? Yes No

Additional Notes:

_____

_____

_____

_____

_____

_____

Greenwich Summer Catamaran Wine Tasting Journal
(For any time of the year)

Date _____
Wine's Name _____
Wine's Producer _____
Winery/Vineyard Location _____
Vintage Year _____
Appearance _____
Aroma _____
Body _____
Taste _____
Finish _____
Would/Does Pair Nicely With _____
Overall Rating From 1-10 _____   Try Again? Yes No

Additional Notes:

_____
_____
_____
_____
_____
_____

Greenwich Summer Catamaran Wine Tasting Journal

(For any time of the year)

Date _____

Wine's Name _____

Wine's Producer _____

Winery/Vineyard Location _____

Vintage Year _____

Appearance _____

Aroma _____

Body _____

Taste _____

Finish _____

Would/Does Pair Nicely With _____

Overall Rating From 1-10 _____   Try Again? Yes No

Additional Notes:

_____

_____

_____

_____

_____

_____

Greenwich Summer Catamaran Wine Tasting Journal
(For any time of the year)

Date _____

Wine's Name _____

Wine's Producer _____

Winery/Vineyard Location _____

Vintage Year _____

Appearance _____

Aroma _____

Body _____

Taste _____

Finish _____

Would/Does Pair Nicely With _____

Overall Rating From 1-10 _____   Try Again? Yes No

Additional Notes:

_____

_____

_____

_____

_____

_____

Greenwich Summer Catamaran Wine Tasting Journal
(For any time of the year)

Date _____

Wine's Name _____

Wine's Producer _____

Winery/Vineyard Location _____

Vintage Year _____

Appearance _____

Aroma _____

Body _____

Taste _____

Finish _____

Would/Does Pair Nicely With _____

Overall Rating From 1-10 _____   Try Again? Yes No

Additional Notes:

_____

_____

_____

_____

_____

_____

Greenwich Summer Catamaran Wine Tasting Journal
(For any time of the year)

Date _____

Wine's Name _____

Wine's Producer _____

Winery/Vineyard Location _____

Vintage Year _____

Appearance _____

Aroma _____

Body _____

Taste _____

Finish _____

Would/Does Pair Nicely With _____

Overall Rating From 1-10 _____   Try Again? Yes No

Additional Notes:

_____

_____

_____

_____

_____

Greenwich Summer Catamaran Wine Tasting Journal
(For any time of the year)

Date _____

Wine's Name _____

Wine's Producer _____

Winery/Vineyard Location _____

Vintage Year _____

Appearance _____

Aroma _____

Body _____

Taste _____

Finish _____

Would/Does Pair Nicely With _____

Overall Rating From 1-10 _____   Try Again? Yes No

Additional Notes:

_____

_____

_____

_____

_____

_____

Greenwich Summer Catamaran Wine Tasting Journal
(For any time of the year)

Date _____

Wine's Name _____

Wine's Producer _____

Winery/Vineyard Location _____

Vintage Year _____

Appearance _____

Aroma _____

Body _____

Taste _____

Finish _____

Would/Does Pair Nicely With _____

Overall Rating From 1-10 _____   Try Again? Yes No

Additional Notes:

_____

_____

_____

_____

_____

_____

Greenwich Summer Catamaran Wine Tasting Journal
(For any time of the year)

Date _____
Wine's Name _____
Wine's Producer _____
Winery/Vineyard Location _____
Vintage Year _____
Appearance _____
Aroma _____
Body _____
Taste _____
Finish _____
Would/Does Pair Nicely With _____
Overall Rating From 1-10 _____   Try Again? Yes No

Additional Notes:

_____
_____
_____
_____
_____

Greenwich Summer Catamaran Wine Tasting Journal
(For any time of the year)

Date _____

Wine's Name _____

Wine's Producer _____

Winery/Vineyard Location _____

Vintage Year _____

Appearance _____

Aroma _____

Body _____

Taste _____

Finish _____

Would/Does Pair Nicely With _____

Overall Rating From 1-10 _____   Try Again? Yes No

Additional Notes:

_____

_____

_____

_____

_____

Greenwich Summer Catamaran Wine Tasting Journal
(For any time of the year)

Date _____
Wine's Name _____
Wine's Producer _____
Winery/Vineyard Location _____
Vintage Year _____
Appearance _____
Aroma _____
Body _____
Taste _____
Finish _____
Would/Does Pair Nicely With _____
Overall Rating From 1-10 _____   Try Again? Yes No

Additional Notes:
_____
_____
_____
_____
_____
_____

Greenwich Summer Catamaran Wine Tasting Journal
(For any time of the year)

Date _____

Wine's Name _____

Wine's Producer _____

Winery/Vineyard Location _____

Vintage Year _____

Appearance _____

Aroma _____

Body _____

Taste _____

Finish _____

Would/Does Pair Nicely With _____

Overall Rating From 1-10 _____   Try Again? Yes No

Additional Notes:

_____

_____

_____

_____

_____

Greenwich Summer Catamaran Wine Tasting Journal
(For any time of the year)

Date _____
Wine's Name _____
Wine's Producer _____
Winery/Vineyard Location _____
Vintage Year _____
Appearance _____
Aroma _____
Body _____
Taste _____
Finish _____
Would/Does Pair Nicely With _____
Overall Rating From 1-10 _____   Try Again? Yes No

Additional Notes:

_____

_____

_____

_____

_____

Greenwich Summer Catamaran Wine Tasting Journal
(For any time of the year)

Date _____
Wine's Name _____
Wine's Producer _____
Winery/Vineyard Location _____
Vintage Year _____
Appearance _____
Aroma _____
Body _____
Taste _____
Finish _____
Would/Does Pair Nicely With _____
Overall Rating From 1-10 _____   Try Again? Yes No

Additional Notes:

_____
_____
_____
_____
_____

Greenwich Summer Catamaran Wine Tasting Journal
(For any time of the year)

Date _____
Wine's Name _____
Wine's Producer _____
Winery/Vineyard Location _____
Vintage Year _____
Appearance _____
Aroma _____
Body _____
Taste _____
Finish _____
Would/Does Pair Nicely With _____
Overall Rating From 1-10 _____   Try Again? Yes No

Additional Notes:

_____
_____
_____
_____
_____

Greenwich Summer Catamaran Wine Tasting Journal
(For any time of the year)

Date _____

Wine's Name _____

Wine's Producer _____

Winery/Vineyard Location _____

Vintage Year _____

Appearance _____

Aroma _____

Body _____

Taste _____

Finish _____

Would/Does Pair Nicely With _____

Overall Rating From 1-10 _____   Try Again? Yes No

Additional Notes:

_____

_____

_____

_____

_____

Greenwich Summer Catamaran Wine Tasting Journal
(For any time of the year)

Date _____
Wine's Name _____
Wine's Producer _____
Winery/Vineyard Location _____
Vintage Year _____
Appearance _____
Aroma _____
Body _____
Taste _____
Finish _____
Would/Does Pair Nicely With _____
Overall Rating From 1-10 _____   Try Again? Yes No

Additional Notes:

_____
_____
_____
_____
_____

Greenwich Summer Catamaran Wine Tasting Journal
(For any time of the year)

Date _____

Wine's Name _____

Wine's Producer _____

Winery/Vineyard Location _____

Vintage Year _____

Appearance _____

Aroma _____

Body _____

Taste _____

Finish _____

Would/Does Pair Nicely With _____

Overall Rating From 1-10 _____   Try Again? Yes No

Additional Notes:

_____

_____

_____

_____

_____

Greenwich Summer Catamaran Wine Tasting Journal
(For any time of the year)

Date _____

Wine's Name _____

Wine's Producer _____

Winery/Vineyard Location _____

Vintage Year _____

Appearance _____

Aroma _____

Body _____

Taste _____

Finish _____

Would/Does Pair Nicely With _____

Overall Rating From 1-10 _____   Try Again? Yes No

Additional Notes:

_____

_____

_____

_____

_____

_____

Greenwich Summer Catamaran Wine Tasting Journal
(For any time of the year)

Date _____

Wine's Name _____

Wine's Producer _____

Winery/Vineyard Location _____

Vintage Year _____

Appearance _____

Aroma _____

Body _____

Taste _____

Finish _____

Would/Does Pair Nicely With _____

Overall Rating From 1-10 _____   Try Again? Yes No

Additional Notes:

_____
_____
_____
_____
_____
_____

Greenwich Summer Catamaran Wine Tasting Journal
(For any time of the year)

Date _____
Wine's Name _____
Wine's Producer _____
Winery/Vineyard Location _____
Vintage Year _____
Appearance _____
Aroma _____
Body _____
Taste _____
Finish _____
Would/Does Pair Nicely With _____
Overall Rating From 1-10 _____   Try Again? Yes No

Additional Notes:

_____
_____
_____
_____
_____
_____

Greenwich Summer Catamaran Wine Tasting Journal
(For any time of the year)

Date _____

Wine's Name _____

Wine's Producer _____

Winery/Vineyard Location _____

Vintage Year _____

Appearance _____

Aroma _____

Body _____

Taste _____

Finish _____

Would/Does Pair Nicely With _____

Overall Rating From 1-10 _____   Try Again? Yes No

Additional Notes:

_____

_____

_____

_____

_____

Greenwich Summer Catamaran Wine Tasting Journal
(For any time of the year)

Date _____

Wine's Name _____

Wine's Producer _____

Winery/Vineyard Location _____

Vintage Year _____

Appearance _____

Aroma _____

Body _____

Taste _____

Finish _____

Would/Does Pair Nicely With _____

Overall Rating From 1-10 _____   Try Again? Yes No

Additional Notes:

_____

_____

_____

_____

_____

Greenwich Summer Catamaran Wine Tasting Journal
(For any time of the year)

Date _____

Wine's Name _____

Wine's Producer _____

Winery/Vineyard Location _____

Vintage Year _____

Appearance _____

Aroma _____

Body _____

Taste _____

Finish _____

Would/Does Pair Nicely With _____

Overall Rating From 1-10 _____   Try Again? Yes No

Additional Notes:

_____

_____

_____

_____

_____

Greenwich Summer Catamaran Wine Tasting Journal
(For any time of the year)

Date _____
Wine's Name _____
Wine's Producer _____
Winery/Vineyard Location _____
Vintage Year _____
Appearance _____
Aroma _____
Body _____
Taste _____
Finish _____
Would/Does Pair Nicely With _____
Overall Rating From 1-10 _____   Try Again? Yes No

Additional Notes:

_____
_____
_____
_____
_____
_____

Greenwich Summer Catamaran Wine Tasting Journal
(For any time of the year)

Date _____

Wine's Name _____

Wine's Producer _____

Winery/Vineyard Location _____

Vintage Year _____

Appearance _____

Aroma _____

Body _____

Taste _____

Finish _____

Would/Does Pair Nicely With _____

Overall Rating From 1-10 _____   Try Again? Yes No

Additional Notes:

_____

_____

_____

_____

_____

Greenwich Summer Catamaran Wine Tasting Journal

(For any time of the year)

Date _____
Wine's Name _____
Wine's Producer _____
Winery/Vineyard Location _____
Vintage Year _____
Appearance _____
Aroma _____
Body _____
Taste _____
Finish _____
Would/Does Pair Nicely With _____
Overall Rating From 1-10 _____   Try Again? Yes No

Additional Notes:

_____
_____
_____
_____
_____
_____

Greenwich Summer Catamaran Wine Tasting Journal
(For any time of the year)

Date _____

Wine's Name _____

Wine's Producer _____

Winery/Vineyard Location _____

Vintage Year _____

Appearance _____

Aroma _____

Body _____

Taste _____

Finish _____

Would/Does Pair Nicely With _____

Overall Rating From 1-10 _____   Try Again? Yes No

Additional Notes:

_____

_____

_____

_____

_____

Greenwich Summer Catamaran Wine Tasting Journal
(For any time of the year)

Date _____
Wine's Name _____
Wine's Producer _____
Winery/Vineyard Location _____
Vintage Year _____
Appearance _____
Aroma _____
Body _____
Taste _____
Finish _____
Would/Does Pair Nicely With _____
Overall Rating From 1-10 _____   Try Again? Yes No

Additional Notes:

_____
_____
_____
_____
_____

Greenwich Summer Catamaran Wine Tasting Journal
(For any time of the year)

Date _____

Wine's Name _____

Wine's Producer _____

Winery/Vineyard Location _____

Vintage Year _____

Appearance _____

Aroma _____

Body _____

Taste _____

Finish _____

Would/Does Pair Nicely With _____

Overall Rating From 1-10 _____   Try Again? Yes No

Additional Notes:

_____

_____

_____

_____

_____

Greenwich Summer Catamaran Wine Tasting Journal

(For any time of the year)

Date _____

Wine's Name _____

Wine's Producer _____

Winery/Vineyard Location _____

Vintage Year _____

Appearance _____

Aroma _____

Body _____

Taste _____

Finish _____

Would/Does Pair Nicely With _____

Overall Rating From 1-10 _____   Try Again? Yes No

Additional Notes:

_____

_____

_____

_____

_____

Greenwich Summer Catamaran Wine Tasting Journal
(For any time of the year)

Date _____
Wine's Name _____
Wine's Producer _____
Winery/Vineyard Location _____
Vintage Year _____
Appearance _____
Aroma _____
Body _____
Taste _____
Finish _____
Would/Does Pair Nicely With _____
Overall Rating From 1-10 _____   Try Again? Yes No

Additional Notes:

_____
_____
_____
_____
_____

Greenwich Summer Catamaran Wine Tasting Journal
(For any time of the year)

Date _____

Wine's Name _____

Wine's Producer _____

Winery/Vineyard Location _____

Vintage Year _____

Appearance _____

Aroma _____

Body _____

Taste _____

Finish _____

Would/Does Pair Nicely With _____

Overall Rating From 1-10 _____   Try Again? Yes No

Additional Notes:

_____

_____

_____

_____

_____

Greenwich Summer Catamaran Wine Tasting Journal
(For any time of the year)

Date _____

Wine's Name _____

Wine's Producer _____

Winery/Vineyard Location _____

Vintage Year _____

Appearance _____

Aroma _____

Body _____

Taste _____

Finish _____

Would/Does Pair Nicely With _____

Overall Rating From 1-10 _____   Try Again? Yes No

Additional Notes:

_____

_____

_____

_____

_____

Greenwich Summer Catamaran Wine Tasting Journal
(For any time of the year)

Date _____

Wine's Name _____

Wine's Producer _____

Winery/Vineyard Location _____

Vintage Year _____

Appearance _____

Aroma _____

Body _____

Taste _____

Finish _____

Would/Does Pair Nicely With _____

Overall Rating From 1-10 _____   Try Again? Yes No

Additional Notes:

_____

_____

_____

_____

_____

Greenwich Summer Catamaran Wine Tasting Journal
(For any time of the year)

Date _____

Wine's Name _____

Wine's Producer _____

Winery/Vineyard Location _____

Vintage Year _____

Appearance _____

Aroma _____

Body _____

Taste _____

Finish _____

Would/Does Pair Nicely With _____

Overall Rating From 1-10 _____   Try Again? Yes No

Additional Notes:

_____

_____

_____

_____

_____

Greenwich Summer Catamaran Wine Tasting Journal
(For any time of the year)

Date _____
Wine's Name _____
Wine's Producer _____
Winery/Vineyard Location _____
Vintage Year _____
Appearance _____
Aroma _____
Body _____
Taste _____
Finish _____
Would/Does Pair Nicely With _____
Overall Rating From 1-10 _____   Try Again? Yes No

Additional Notes:

_____
_____
_____
_____
_____

Greenwich Summer Catamaran Wine Tasting Journal
(For any time of the year)

Date _____

Wine's Name _____

Wine's Producer _____

Winery/Vineyard Location _____

Vintage Year _____

Appearance _____

Aroma _____

Body _____

Taste _____

Finish _____

Would/Does Pair Nicely With _____

Overall Rating From 1-10 _____   Try Again? Yes No

Additional Notes:

_____

_____

_____

_____

_____

Greenwich Summer Catamaran Wine Tasting Journal

(For any time of the year)

Date _____

Wine's Name _____

Wine's Producer _____

Winery/Vineyard Location _____

Vintage Year _____

Appearance _____

Aroma _____

Body _____

Taste _____

Finish _____

Would/Does Pair Nicely With _____

Overall Rating From 1-10 _____   Try Again? Yes No

Additional Notes:

_____

_____

_____

_____

_____

Greenwich Summer Catamaran Wine Tasting Journal
(For any time of the year)

Date _____

Wine's Name _____

Wine's Producer _____

Winery/Vineyard Location _____

Vintage Year _____

Appearance _____

Aroma _____

Body _____

Taste _____

Finish _____

Would/Does Pair Nicely With _____

Overall Rating From 1-10 _____   Try Again? Yes No

Additional Notes:

_____

_____

_____

_____

_____

Greenwich Summer Catamaran Wine Tasting Journal
(For any time of the year)

Date _____

Wine's Name _____

Wine's Producer _____

Winery/Vineyard Location _____

Vintage Year _____

Appearance _____

Aroma _____

Body _____

Taste _____

Finish _____

Would/Does Pair Nicely With _____

Overall Rating From 1-10 _____   Try Again? Yes No

Additional Notes:

_____
_____
_____
_____
_____

Greenwich Summer Catamaran Wine Tasting Journal
(For any time of the year)

Date _____

Wine's Name _____

Wine's Producer _____

Winery/Vineyard Location _____

Vintage Year _____

Appearance _____

Aroma _____

Body _____

Taste _____

Finish _____

Would/Does Pair Nicely With _____

Overall Rating From 1-10 _____   Try Again? Yes No

Additional Notes:

_____

_____

_____

_____

_____

Greenwich Summer Catamaran Wine Tasting Journal
(For any time of the year)

Date _____
Wine's Name _____
Wine's Producer _____
Winery/Vineyard Location _____
Vintage Year _____
Appearance _____
Aroma _____
Body _____
Taste _____
Finish _____
Would/Does Pair Nicely With _____
Overall Rating From 1-10 _____   Try Again? Yes No

Additional Notes:

_____
_____
_____
_____
_____
_____

Greenwich Summer Catamaran Wine Tasting Journal
(For any time of the year)

Date _____
Wine's Name _____
Wine's Producer _____
Winery/Vineyard Location _____
Vintage Year _____
Appearance _____
Aroma _____
Body _____
Taste _____
Finish _____
Would/Does Pair Nicely With _____
Overall Rating From 1-10 _____   Try Again? Yes No

Additional Notes:

_____
_____
_____
_____
_____

www.ingramcontent.com/pod-product-compliance
Lightning Source LLC
Chambersburg PA
CBHW050320120526
44592CB00014B/1982